Series 536

This is a book to read before you go on holiday, and a book to take with you on holiday. It will help you to find, and to name, some of the interesting animals and plants you will find on the seashore—animals and plants you will find nowhere else in the town or country.

It will also tell you where to find them on the seashore, and that is important. All seashore animals have special parts of the shore in which they prefer to live; it would be no use, for instance, looking for a lug worm up on the rocks because it lives buried in the wet sand. Nor would it be any use looking for a limpet in the wet sand, because it lives on the rocks.

But you will not make these mistakes after you have read this book, because you will KNOW where to look.

THE SEASHORE
and Seashore Life

by NANCY SCOTT

with illustrations by
JILL PAYNE

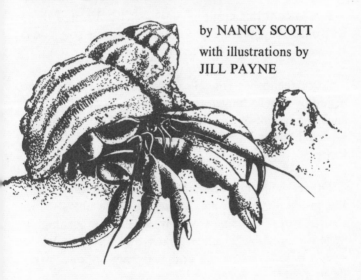

Publishers : Ladybird Books Ltd . Loughborough
© Ladybird Books Ltd (formerly Wills & Hepworth Ltd) 1964
Printed in England

THE SEASHORE AND SEASHORE LIFE

How enjoyable it is to scramble over the seaweed-strewn rocks; to lie on the firm sand in the warm sun; to swim in the sparkling sea, and to go for a boat trip round the harbour.

But stop! Is that all there is at the seaside—just rocks, sand, sea and boats? Of course not. Why, the seashore is the home ground of more animals than any other part of the countryside.

Just look at this group of empty shells. Each of these was once the covering of an animal with a soft body. It needed this tough shell as protection.

Some shellfishes are called bivalves because they live inside two shells hinged together. The large fan-shaped shell is one-half of a bivalve, it is the Cockle which lives buried in the soft wet sand in the low-water area of the shore.

Other shellfishes are called univalves because they live inside one shell only. There are some univalves in the picture (the small yellow shells, for example). When a univalve is under water and alive, it moves over the sea bed, rocks and seaweeds on one large, fleshy foot.

The other shells will be described later on.

4

0 7214 0103 1

Walk quietly on the wet sands as the tide goes out and watch for tiny jets of water spurting into the air. These come from the long Razor shell. It is sometimes called a 'spout fish' because of this spouting habit.

Can you see the Razor in the picture—it is half buried in the sand just below the Scallop shell. The Razor Shell can burrow very quickly and deeply down into the wet sand. It has a long fleshy foot which it pushes downwards, then it grips the sand and pulls its long shell down after it. Feel how smooth the shell is. Now you will understand why it slips down so easily and quickly.

Scallop shells live in the sea all the time. The fully grown Scallop can swim about by clapping the two-halves of its shell together. This is a useful accomplishment as it means that the Scallop can escape from its enemies, and also move to another part of the sea where food may be more plentiful.

The Scallop also has eyes, many of them. You can only see them when its shells are open, and then they look like a row of glistening jewels just below the rim of the upper shell. Each one has a well-developed focusing lens, a retina and nerve fibres.

To see live Periwinkles you must explore the rocks, breakwaters and pier pilings at low tide. They eat tiny pieces of seaweed, so you will find them wherever seaweed is growing.

The Small Periwinkle is very tiny indeed, about the size of the tip of your little finger. You can see a few at the bottom of the picture.

The Rough Periwinkles have fine raised lines all over them, and a sharply marked spiral. You can feel these if you touch them.

The Common Periwinkle has a thicker shell than the others. This is the shellfish called Winkles which you buy in the fishshops, or off the stalls on the promenade.

The delicate yellow and pink shells are the Flat Periwinkles, the prettiest of all the periwinkle shells to add to your collection. If you examine the seaweed fronds closely you may find some of the eggs of this particular periwinkle. It lays a cluster of eggs together inside a blob of jelly which holds them firmly fastened on to the seaweed.

Under the covering of long seaweed fronds, and clinging to the rocks at the low tide level, you will find the Common Whelk, sometimes called a Buckie.

Do you see that big ball-shaped spongy-looking object? That is a batch of the Common Whelk's egg-cases. They are empty now because the baby whelks have hatched out in the sea, but the sea has washed up the egg-cases for you to find and examine.

The sea washes up many other interesting things for you to find, particularly shells, but the animals themselves when alive lived deep down in the sand, or at the lowest tide level, so you may never see them alive.

To the left of the Whelk's egg-cases are two tiny Cowries, dainty little shells rarely more than half-an-inch long. On tropical seashores Cowries grow bigger than your hand.

Below the Cowries is a Sunset shell. You can always tell this from the others because of its 'sunset rays'.

The other shells are Tellins, with very delicately marked, thin shells.

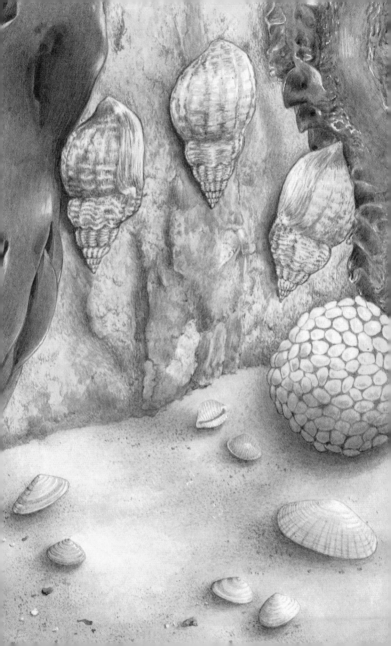

Have you heard people say 'it sticks like a limpet'? They mean that something is so firmly fixed they cannot move it.

Well, if you try to move a Limpet shell off a rock, you will quickly understand this saying, for the Limpets on the edge of this rock pool are each holding on to the rock with an extremely strong foot, and even the roughest waves or the hardest pull will not move them. But when the sea covers them, then they can walk freely on their one foot.

They walk across the rock, eating the tiny short seaweeds. Then the tide turns, and each Limpet knows that it is time to return home; and the amazing thing is that each one of these Limpets will return to the exact spot on the rock that it left awhile ago, and settle down firmly into the slight grooves it has made with the edges of its shell in the rock face.

If you walk quietly up to a limpet-covered rock you will see some of the Limpets peeping—just as some of them are doing in our picture. But the slightest vibration near the rock will make them clamp down harder than ever.

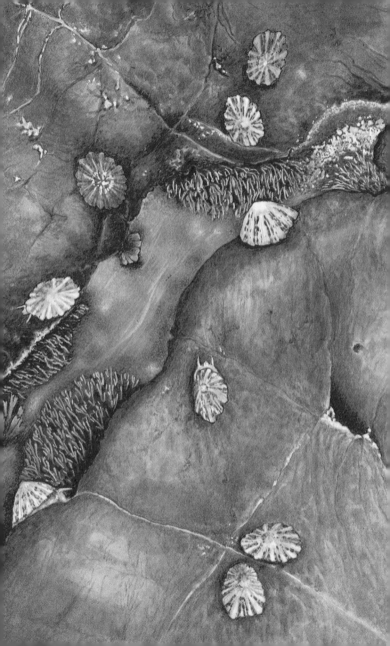

Another shell that 'sticks like a limpet' is the Barnacle. These are smaller than the Limpets.

They stick to the rocks, pier piles and jetty supports, and they never move away, not even to feed as the Limpets do. Instead they feed by opening a little doorway in the peak of their cone and pushing out a bunch of fine bristles with which they catch their food from the water when the tide is in.

Lower down the pier piles and on the rocks live the Mussels. They, too, never move away from home, but they do not cling to their anchorage by a foot. The Mussels have a special way of holding on. Each one secretes from a special gland in its foot a large number of silken threads called byssus, and with these they tether themselves to the rocks; but the threads are long enough to allow the mussels to move with the ebb and flow of the water, because it is essential for the water to flow freely through the two parts of the shell. As the water flows through the shell, the Mussels pick out their food, and take in fresh oxygen.

In the little pools left at the foot of the pier piles, breakwaters, and in some of the big, sandy pools, lives the tiny Shrimp.

At first you may have difficulty in spotting this little Shrimp because its colour tones in so well with the sand, and not only that, but this seashore animal spends most of the day partly buried in the sand with just its little black eyes showing. You can see one buried like this at the bottom of the picture.

But sometimes even its eyes are hidden. However, if you disturb the sand a little and watch closely you will see one or more dart away to find another spot to hide in. You can then watch it burrow into the sand, which it does by sinking backwards and then pushing more sand over its back with its long feelers.

If you see a Shrimp with a mass of spotted, frothy-looking stuff clinging to the swimming appendages below its body, then that is a female Shrimp carrying her eggs about with her. She holds them together like this until they are ready to hatch out, usually for about four weeks.

The Lug Worm at the bottom of the picture lives in a U-shaped burrow which it lines with a mucus from its body to strengthen the walls. It swallows sand and from the sand it takes the tiny particles of food it needs. The sand it does not want it leaves outside one end of its burrow in little coiled casts. The other end of its burrow is in that little pit by the worm's head.

Behind the Lug Worm is the tube home of the Peacock Worm, with its crown of brightly coloured tentacles spread out at the top to catch its food. It is from these handsome gills the Peacock Worm gets its name, although its body is also brightly coloured in shades of pale green with a tinted tail of orange or violet.

But the tube home made by this worm (and the one at the top of the picture—the Sand Mason) is one of the greatest wonders of the seashore world, for each of these worms constructs its tubular home from tiny particles of sand, shell or mud glued together with a sticky mucus from its own body. You may never see either of these handsome worms alive, as when the tide is out they retreat right down into the bottom section of their long burrows, but you will certainly see the tops of their homes if they are living on the particular shore you are exploring—when the tide is out they look like tufts of bristles sticking up out of the sand.

Take care when you are climbing over seaweed covered rocks, for the seaweed is wet and very slippery. When Bladder Wrack is dry, you can have great fun popping its bladders. These bladders are filled with a gas which helps the weed to float freely in the water, so leaving space below it for other seaweeds, such as the Knotted Wrack, and particularly the animals, to move about. When the sea covers these rocks the world below is a vast seaweed forest full of swimming, walking and crawling animals.

Those long strips like leather shoe laces on the sand below, are Thong Weed.

Do you see the disc-shaped piece in the centre of this mass of Thong Weed? This is its hold-fast. Seaweeds do not need roots as they get all their food directly from the sea, but they do need something with which to anchor themselves firmly to the rocks and stones or they would be washed up on to dry land and die. So each plant develops a strong sucker-disc at its base and with this it clasps the rocky surface.

Explore the rocks and seaweed covered stones, and you will see the different shapes and thicknesses of these holdfasts.

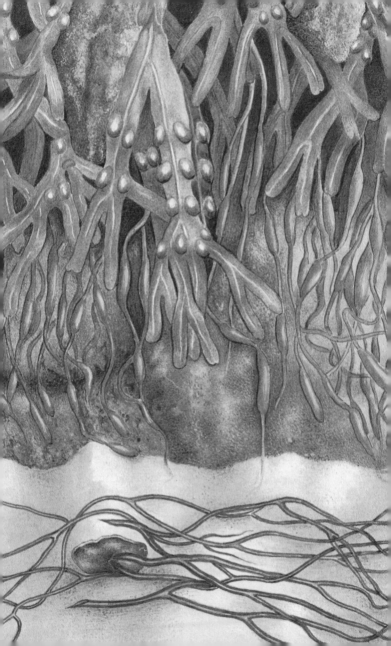

Watch the fishes swimming in and out of the seaweed in a pool. If you are exploring a pool near the high water mark you may see the small three-spined Stickleback shown at the top of our picture. You can also see this Stickleback in ponds and canals inland. But you will never see its cousin, the fifteen-spined Stickleback, with a longer, slimmer body, in inland waters, as it is a marine fish only. But both species have the same interesting breeding habits.

The male builds a neat little cave-like nest by binding together seaweeds with gluey threads formed within his own body. Then he chooses his mate who lays her eggs inside the nest, and then away she swims leaving the male Stickleback to guard the eggs until they hatch out.

He is very brave and ferocious in his guarding, too, and will chase off other preying animals two and three times his own size.

Another fish that guards his eggs is the Shanny, or Common Blenny, at the bottom of our picture. This is the fish you will see darting so quickly from side to side in the pools.

The Common or Sand Goby is an even better father. He carefully scoops out a little cave under a stone or an empty shell, and then the female fastens the eggs to the roof of the cave. She may lay two or three hundred eggs at a time.

Now the father Sand Goby not only stands guard, but also he spends hours and hours swishing fresh water in and out of the nest with his fins. In this way he aerates the water surrounding the eggs and also keeps them clean.

If the stone or shell is moved to another part of the pool, he will follow it, promptly scoop more sand over it, then dig another tunnel and take up his guarding, fanning position again.

The Sand Goby is very small, about two to three inches long, and when heavy seas tumble roughly into the pools he would have a bad time of it, if it was not for a clever little adaptation to his paired hind-fins. These are joined together to form a fan-shaped sucker-disc, and with this sucker the little Goby can cling to the rocks until the water in the pool calms down again.

Of course you will see crabs in the rock pools and on the shore.

A crab has five pairs of legs. The front pair have strong pincers on them, and they will nip your toes if you get too near!

Crabs are the only animals that scuttle sideways, pulling with one set of legs and pushing with the other.

You will find many empty crab shells on the beach. These are not dead crabs, only the casing a crab has grown out of just as we grow out of our clothes and shoes. You see, the crab's body is soft and has no skeleton, so—like the shellfish—it needs a protective covering. This covering is called a carapace. The crab's body grows, but its carapace does not. So at regular intervals, while it is growing, the crab throws off this too-tight shell, and then has to wait a while for its new carapace—which has been forming beneath the old one—to stretch and harden. While its new carapace is hardening the crab has to hide; if it did not it would soon be gobbled up by a hungry seagull or a fish.

The green crab is the Shore Crab which you will find on nearly all shores. The red one at the bottom of the picture is a young Edible Crab—you will never see a fully-grown Edible Crab on the shore, they live in the deep sea. The middle one is a Swimming Crab.

26

You will need sharp eyes to spot the Spider Crabs hiding among the seaweeds, as you can tell by the well hidden Long Legged Spider Crab in our picture. If this was the Common Spider Crab you would not be able to see it at all, as it has hook-like projections all over its small body, and on these it attaches tiny fragments of seaweed or sponges, and in this way hides itself even more securely away from searching eyes and possible danger.

The other crab in our picture is a tiny Hairy Porcelain Crab. You will have to search under stones and the lower parts of the rocks for these, as they spend most of their life gripping the hard surface with the sharply pointed spines on the ends of their walking legs. This is the way they protect themselves from being washed away by the waves.

They can swim if they want to, swimming backwards like a lobster, but they prefer to cling and slither about on the stones.

The mud collects on the hair on their legs, and this also helps to camouflage them from their enemies.

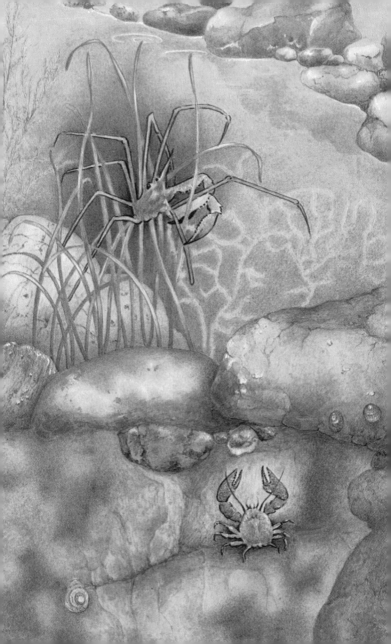

But there is one crab which has no thick shell of its own to protect its body, so it has to find the empty shell of another sea animal to live in. This is the Hermit Crab. If you see a whelk or a winkle shell which seems to be walking across the bottom of a pool on legs, then you have found a Hermit Crab.

The Hermit in our picture is about to change 'homes' as he has now grown too big for his old shell. He is exploring another empty, but larger, whelk shell. He will feel that shell all over most carefully, inside and out, and he will not attempt to pull his body out of his old shell until he is quite sure that the new one is exactly right in size and shape.

When he does decide, he will then feel with his long antennae all round the shell as far away and up as possible to make certain that there are no enemies lurking nearby to snatch up his soft body. If he feels it is safe to make the move he will grip the new shell, and with a surprisingly quick movement withdraw his body and flick it over and into the new shell, curling his soft body around the central pillar of the shell to hold himself securely in position.

One of the Hermit's claws is bigger than the other. When it gets right down inside the shell, it uses this big claw to close up the opening, just like a strong front door.

Do you see those small blobs of jelly sticking to the wet rocks at the top of the picture? They are Sea Anemones.

Now look down into the pool and see them under water. Something wonderful has happened: each little blob has opened out into a 'flower', but the petals are called tentacles, and each tentacle is armed with innumerable poisonous stinging cells—the Sea Anemone uses these tentacles to catch its food, for the Sea Anemone is a flesh-eating animal, not a plant as its name implies.

Watch, and you will see these tentacles capture some food, perhaps a small crab, a tiny shrimp or a periwinkle. It will push its prey into its mouth which is in the centre of its body. Then it will close up to eat its meal. Presently it will open up again and spit out the hard parts of the meal—small pieces of crab carapace or a tiny periwinkle shell. The Anemone cannot digest hard food.

The red and yellow Anemones are Beadlets, and these can be found wherever there are some rocks to cling to. Each Beadlet will have about two hundred fine tentacles.

Below, on the left, are two Opelets, sometimes called Snake-locks. They also have about two hundred tentacles, but the one next to them, the Dahlia, only has about eighty tentacles. Not that this makes it any less deadly to the small swimming sea animals.

32

Those big blobs of jelly you sometimes find on the beach are Jellyfishes. A Jellyfish is nearly all water and so it will dry up quickly in the sun.

It is not wise to touch them with your hand or your bare foot as some Jellyfishes have a slight irritant on their bodies which can have unpleasant effects on human flesh.

But, if you find a Jellyfish, you can gently scoop it up in a pail and tip it into a rock pool. Then, if it is still alive, you will see its frills and long trailing tentacles. These tentacles are used in the same way as the Anemones use theirs—to catch their food. The Jellyfish swims by opening and closing its large dome in the same way as you flick open and close an umbrella.

The tiny floating balls are Sea Gooseberries. These are often washed up on the shore, and they look like oval glass marbles. When they are swimming you can see their two long fishing-line tentacles. These are sticky and so when a small sea animal touches one of them, it adheres, and then the Sea Gooseberry hauls in his fishing line, bringing the captive into his mouth.

The real name of the Sea Gooseberry is Ctenophora.

If the Starfish loses an arm, it can grow a new one.

Under these arms it has rows of tiny tube feet with suckers on them which help it to move about, and to get its food. On top it has dozens of small pincers that twist and turn all ways; these grip and throw off the specks of sand, shell scraps, mud, and any other unwanted rubbish which would soon bury the Starfish if not cleared away.

It has a very tiny mouth right in the centre of its body, and no teeth, so it can only eat soft food.

You could hold the small Cushion Star on the left in your hand quite easily. But you would need a large pail to hold the bigger Stars, as they may be anything from six to twenty inches across from arm-tip to arm-tip.

The delicate Brittle Stars at the top are extremely well-named, as their arms are so brittle they snap off at the slightest touch; so it is a good thing they have that marvellous power of growing new limbs when needed. Their tube-feet have no suckers on them, instead they rely on the sinuous movements of their arms to get about.

That grey oval-shaped object on the lower right is the empty case of a Heart Sea Urchin. By the time you find it, the sea and the sand will have worn off most of its spines, but when it was alive it was covered with them—like the one at the top of the picture. You may see one alive, and moving about, in a rock pool.

Pick up an empty case and look for the tiny holes between the remaining spines. These held its long slender tube feet, and its nippers which it used to help gather food, and clear unwanted rubbish from its body—just like the Starfish, for the Sea Urchin belongs to the same family as the Starfish.

The mouth of the Sea Urchin is underneath its body, and in it are five big beak-like teeth which it uses to scrape off the tiny seaweeds on which it feeds.

At the top of the page is the Common Sea Urchin. Notice how its spines stick out in all directions. Now look at the fully-spined Heart Urchin and you will see that this Urchin's spines all point the same way. This is because the Heart Urchin burrows into the sand, and if its spines stuck out all ways, as do those of the Common Sea Urchin, it would have great difficulty in burrowing.

After a rough sea you may find Mermaid's Purses washed up on the shore.

This is a fanciful name for the egg cases of certain big fishes that live in the deepest parts of the sea. A baby Skate hatched out of the black one, and a baby Dogfish out of the brown one.

Do you see the long and curly points at each corner? Once these tendrils were soft and pliable. They curled around seaweeds growing on the sea bed under water, and in this way the egg cases were held, safely moored in place, until the baby fish hatched out.

Can you pick out the shells in the picture? There is a Razor, three different Periwinkles, and a small Cockle; but these are only a few of the interesting shells, and other strange things, you will find on a seashore after a heavy sea.

If you find something that looks like a piece of dark felt about the size of your hand, you have found a Sea Mouse. It usually lives buried in the sand on the sea bed.

Of course it is not a mouse at all, any more than the Sea Gooseberry was a gooseberry. It is really a worm, a scale-worm, because its body is covered in scales. These scales are in turn covered by a mat of fine hairs, and if you wash your Sea Mouse in sea water and then hold it under the water you will see the wonderful colours of its hair, just as they are in the picture.

That small shell at the bottom of the picture, looking like a tiny doll's cradle, is a Slipper Limpet. Some children call them Boat Limpets. They do not live on the rocks like the other limpets, but instead they cling one on top of the other. You will see a pile of them above the Sea Mouse.

Perhaps you can find some seaside jewels among the pebbles and rocks.

The best time to look for them is when the tide is going out and the sun is shining, for then they sparkle and show up in their finest colours.

A great many of the semi-precious stones used in the make-up of pieces of jewellery, necklaces, brooches, ear-rings and rings for your fingers, come from the seashore.

The white one is called Rock Crystal. The purple one is Amethyst.

That pretty pink piece is Rose Quartz, and the variegated striped ones are Onyx.

Some of the pebbles are very pretty and worth collecting, too. With these, and the shells you have been gathering, you can build up an attractive and interesting collection of seaside specimens. The best way to house your collection is to divide up a shallow drawer or several large dress boxes into small sections. Then you can place one specimen in each section, name it and add the name of the shore where it was found.

If you lift up the driftweed along the high tide line a cloud of little shrimp-like creatures will hop up.

These are Sand-hoppers. When they are resting under the dead weed their bodies are bent. But when you lift up the weed and startle them they straighten their bodies suddenly and this is what makes them appear to hop.

These seashore animals, although so tiny, perform a useful service on the seashore as they eat up a great deal of the decaying and rotting matter which would otherwise make the seashore very unpleasant at times.

Can you see that little creature sheltering in the crack in the breakwater which is just above the high tide mark. That is a Common Sea Slater.

The Sea Slaters come out at night to feed, as they do not like the daylight, or even very bright moonlight. The reason for this is that the seabirds would soon spot them scuttling about on the dry shore in the daytime, but at night they are safe from such enemies.

Both the Sand-hopper and the Sea Slater are much sought-after as foods by the birds, so both animals keep well hidden as long as possible.

As you enjoy yourself on the sand and in the sea the Gulls will be flying overhead all the time. Notice how graceful they are, and how surely they fly in and out, and over and above one another. You never see two birds collide with one another in mid-air, no matter how many there may be together.

If you are eating they will often land quite close to you, hoping you will throw them some scraps. It is much easier to snap up a crust of bread or a tasty snippet of cake than to search for a live shellfish, or a sandworm!

The large black and white Herring Gulls in our picture are the adult birds, the speckled brown and white one is a young bird under five years old.

The gulls make their rough nests on the ledges of the cliffs, and often their nests will be right in the heart of a clump of Sea Pink, or Thrift as many people call it. They seem to like to make their nests among these flowers.

Most of the gulls lay two or three eggs in May or June, so if you want to see the parents feeding the young chicks you must visit the coast in June or July.

That big black and white bird standing on one leg is an Oyster-Catcher. She makes her nest among the pebbles and rocks above the high tide line. Her nest is called a scrape because it is merely a small hollow scraped out of the sand and pebbles. The eggs look just like the pebbles around the nest and so are very hard to find—this is the way she hides her eggs. The chicks are also speckly and hard to spot on the seashore.

Notice the Oyster-Catcher's long, probing beak. This is one of the few seabirds which can dislodge a limpet. It stands on a rock covered with limpets and waits quietly until a limpet is 'peeping', then with a swift, sharp, sideways blow with its long beak it sends the limpet bowling off the rock. To the left of this bird is a prickly plant called Sea-Holly.

The smaller bird is a Turnstone, and it really does turn stones over. Watch, and you will see it doing this. It is searching for sand-hoppers and insects to eat.

The Marram Grass growing among the sand above the high tide line, and among the dunes, holds the sand together and stops it being washed away into the sea by the rain.

INDEX OF SEASHORE LIFE